SENSUOUS SEDUCTION WITH SHADOWS

A COLLECTION OF POETRY

ANUPMA SHARMA

ISBN 979-8-89186-420-7

Foreword

Dear Reader,

Come join me in affirmation, affection and adventure through a journey on Sensuous Seduction with Shadows.

My name is Ms. Anupma Sharma and I am an author who enjoys the debacles and challenges of creative exploration. This poetry collection is the tip of the iceberg of my work. It is a culmination of Four years of work of sensitivity towards sustainable development. It is an attempt of preservation for posterity. I first had the opportunity to write when I was only ten. An attack by the bull on a Saturday scheduled for a walk made me pen the escapade in the newsletter. The bull raged not because of the red colour of the jerkin that we wore but the movement as I found out years later. The bull is colour blind to red. We were subsumed with fright only to laugh in hindsight.

Here children will dabble and dialogue as they tread across a wondrous path of pacifying their quelling of knowledge for a conquest for eternity.

I have published a poetry book **Horizons – A Journey Far Traversed in 2015 under the ageism of Partridge**. It is a collection besotted by my childhood memories luring the child into musical melodies that are like a rhapsody.

Sensuous Seduction with Shadows is a collection magical moments reflecting myriad moods that are astride.

Acknowledgement

This collection is dedicated to my parents, for their support, sensitivity and sobriety through turbulent times. My sister Manisha a pearl in an oyster and my sister Anuradha a drop in the vast ocean making a difference.

For Sharan in keeping the faith alive!

For Agastya's agility that inspired provocative, patient and perseverant thoughts that made me pen a penchant for a unique paradigm.

For Versatile Viraaj, Chase your dreams like the wind beneath your wings and to Rahul for just being there.

For Arunima and Jay may this piece seal the magic between you.

Contents

Contents

Come Dazzle and Dribble with Children

Come Challenge the Debacles of the Mind

Ancient Wonders of the World – Come Preserve and Protect for Posterity

Egypt to the Fore

Conclusion – A Penchant for Peace

Come Steal Magical, Mesmerizing, Moments

1. Magic Seduction

A sunset so splendor

Creating magic and wonder

Oh! Love,

Come hold me in your arms

That is yonder

Feel the passion subsumed in surrender

Feel the surrender that is eroded by a blunder.

A blunder that is a plunder

Oh! Plunder rise above the past

Search for the passion fore cast.

Come let the passion seduce you,

With magical moments, mesmerizing you.

A kiss,

A touch,

A benediction

For a resurrection of love

2. Pleasure

Oh! Love

How do I subsume our lust into a desire?

The validity,

The verse and

The verdict is questionable

Let us rejoice in a prayer for resilience

Restoration and

Refurbishment of a cry from the heart

Till the lark sings a song

To besiege the moment

Besotted with true love.

A pleasure so pure,

A pleasure paramount,

A pleasure surmount

Like a symphony,

A melody surpass and a cacophony not so sure of the past.

3. Magical Liaison

To you my love is the love everlasting

A hug;

A caress and a

Brush as tender as a butterfly.

It is evocative,

It is erotic and

It is like an aphrodisiac.

A touch of a hand

Blossoming like ethereal magic

Serene,

Seductive

Putting superstition to shame.

Today I surrender to you,

In everlasting jubilation and joy,

Both juxtaposed over one another.

4. Yearning

Oh! How much I yearn for your love.

To hold and to touch

For a crimson flush,

The depth of my soul

Calls for you

Can you hear me?

In resonance

A plight of a wounded heart,

In cognizance with a resurrection,

A resurrection of my soul;

Today is a new dawn,

Today is the rebound of tomorrow,

Alas! Today is you and I

In love, in lust and a liaison so complete

5. Forest

A lull before the storm,

Mingling with the forest at bay.

The aura and the aroma tiding over a turbulent day,

The evergreen forest

Is here to set us apart.

The autumn leaves dance like a ballerina

The spring flowers shower their blessing.

Fire flamed autumn strike a chord in the heart

That is succinct and tricky

Giving up caution to the wind.

6. Forest on Flames

As I walk on the wild side of love

I see the forest on flame,

A flame of desire,

Passionate,

Pensive yet a proclamation;

A proclamation to a head-start fusion of love;

Memorable,

Acclamation with accolades

To none other than our fate;

A kiss to kindle a heart beat away;

Just like a fire

Burning like a furnace of desire.

A benediction in solace,

Shimmering like flames,

Of an acoustics cutting like a double-edged knife

7. Captivity

Look! Love captivated
How you have captured my soul.
My benediction calls for freedom.
Freedom from servitude
Freedom from anarchy
Above all freedom from chaotic disorder,
This is a lesson of a liaison,
Of trust
Triumph and a fall of tyranny
The touch of bodies meeting in a fire,
Igniting a flame of desire
To break through the captivity;
Come join in assimilation through dedication,
defiance
And a semblance of a different love.

8. Ardent Desire

They walked hand in hand
Love and lust,
Ardent amok a pinnacle of a leisure
To a disclosure that ended in a closure;
A love blatant so pure
A lust reclining to sheer passion,
Passion aghast to be subsumed in pathos of igniting
Fervor;
Today I surrender to my love
Making love in the moon lit night,
The liaison is strong
With surrender absolved.
Love s blind precursor to the lust
Lust that is a sexual desire.

9. Flamenco

Are you lone-some?

Are you lack luster?

Or

Are you ahead of your times?

Exotic, exuberant and erotic

A blend of all

Where I dance to flamenco

One step forward two steps backward

Here we have a tango of two

The flower sacred and the dance seductive

One Spanish Harlem

The other waiting in the wings for

Accolades, and applause

A swing, a sway

A twirl another way

10. Remembrance

A song, a melody setting the memory free
Of a sun-set so splendor
Seclusion for the lust
A remembrance of the crimson flush
From dawn to dusk
It was an arid of songs
Astride with gypsies in a caravan
Singing to ethereal bliss
Reinforcing surrender
Trying to remember
Love,
A song a melody setting the memory free
To catapult the remembrance of love and lust

11. Lyrical Love

As I stand by the moonlit night
I hear a musical tune
Like a melody forlorn;
An ecstasy
A profane moment of recollection
Restoration and
Re-jubilation.
The lyrics were many
Like a symphony so dear
To a heart full of cheer;
The musical melody was astride a personification on
A bleak night
To challenge by right
The fear in hindsight
Full of disdain in vain
Come join in affirmation and affection through
Association of lyrical love

12. Illicit-Affair

I longed for his touch,
It was like the touch of a child.
Innocent, ambiguous and an aperture of the lust;
It was an illicit affair
Like a forbidden fruit,
Challenging the liaison
Only to be subsumed by the affair;
Unaccepted yet daring
A call for surrender
A haul of my destiny
Alas! One to be claimed as an illicit affair

13. Girl of Today

A girl so vibrant,
A girl so vivacious,
An epitome of a challenge;
To simply follow a path
It is like a hue of a rainbow
The seven sisters in a tow;
Cheerfully challenging the moments
Of life's escapades,
Till death do us apart
The girl of today
Is the helm of tomorrow
This story is narrated, by none other than a
Sutradhar;
Today is paramount,
Today is pervasive and
Today is an everlasting tale.

14. Love and Lust

Love is a desire

Love is a treasure and love is a passion.

On the other hand lust is a craving

Compounded with the soul into the culmination of
a simple blush,

Making one wonder in awe of it all

Oh! The blush was like a first crush,

Erratic,

Exuberant and

Exciting without the luster of the lust.

15. Dangerous Liaison

As I woke up to the sunrise

I peered to see the dawn of a new day.

There is a liaison

A liaison between dawn and dusk

One bright and beautiful

Another dark and dusky

With hues, all the way

Let us capture the ethereal bliss

Breaking into the monotony.

One a sunrise another sunset

An amelioration of the moon and the stars

Can you spot a shooting star?

A dangerous liaison

In the planets set afar;

Each trying to surpass that other,

In beauty and bounty in the sky above

16. Flying Kiss

She came like a breath of fresh air,

And mingled beyond compare.

The flight of the kiss was,

Like a brush of a feather in the moonlit night;

Her name was the flying kiss.

It came out of a touch of the hand and the lips,

To rest on the shoulder of a prince;

To resolutely defy

The rules of the game,

She brought joy,

She brought happiness above all she brought a
smile

To the destined lips

17. A Benediction

Today I make a benediction

A simple prayer;

To be subtle and sensuous

In every move I make.

A kiss

A caress and an igniting flame for love.

A prayer

A jolt from within;

Where horizons meet,

Meet in passive resistance

Looking to be cheerful and gay.

The sun the precursor,

The moon in surreal surrender,

Both a culmination towards

Ethereal,

Exotic and exuberant way of life

18. Tip Toe

As I tip toe in the bed room
I see my lover in a slumber.
Deep and sound without a doubt;
I look at him,
I stare wide - eyed
At the crimson flush,
It seemed like a blush
His eyes open
To see me standing in the recluse
To smile in surrender;
We touch,
We kiss
And hold each other close in surrender
Love is here,
To tip toe in our hearts

19. A Rider

A rider who was a riddle,
A rebel in the making,
Elusive yet evocative;
Taking cognizance of the ride
Banished from sight.
An epitome of surrender
To the sacrosanct sanctuary of desire
The surrender to this desire;
To ride,
To subscribe and
To surmount the fear,
Like the destined equestrian so dear

20. Passion

As I sit under the stars
With my lover in the stark,
There is no delusion
But the pure passion
Flowing through my veins.
We kiss,
We hold each other close,
Kindling the flame of devotion.
The touch is ethereal;
Submissive to devotion
Full of bounty,
Subsumed in integrity.
Passion flows like a stream entwined
Entwined in an enigma
Over flowing with charisma
Passion is sublime
Subservient and sensual
In this quest of love and passion forlorn

21. Love

As I stood under the setting sun
I saw my love reining in,
Reclining like dew drops
On a rose bud,
Waiting to shimmer in all glory.
The petals told a tale;
Leaving a trail behind
A sadness for some,
While an ecstasy for many;
Love is retribution,
Love is a reconciliation and
Love a force to reckon with.

22. Flame

As the lamp burnt at midnight
It released a fire,
That is like a desire.
Submissive and silent
Subsumed with love.
An ache that is heart wrenching,
A passion that is a flame,
A flame that ignites,
A flame that subsides and
A flame that is an intoxication of love;
A love that is eye catching
A flame that is soul searching and withstanding
Withstanding the test of time.

23. Sensuality

Oh! Love, come, hold me
In sensual surrender,
In a cast astute with wonder
An awe of abysmal hunger
A touch,
A benediction and
A supreme surrender.
A rejoicing of life
Like a collateral of a tide.
Come uphold this love
Don't cave in by the thunder.
A call for
Brave, buoyant and blissful way
giving into sensuality.
The touch ethereal
The lovemaking a tirade of joy
A call for blossoming like a flower in hindsight.

24. Femme Fatale'

Femme fatale' miraculously

Bold and beautiful

A seductress

A temptress

Full of aura and lure;

A bargain for money

A liaison of the soul

Looking out for knight in shining armor.

A link in the chain

Of a lover in vain.

She was tactful to the core,

Looking to the heavens to cajole

For the French she was a "disastrous woman"

Mysterious, melodramatic and mischievous

A dare to bare catapult by some as 'woman archaic'

Yet shaking the pendulum to come to the fore.

A simple prayer in search of a liaison of love and lust

Leading and lending an intrigue to sexuality

The old-fashioned way

25. Eyes

Those eyes are daring,
Those eyes are daunting,
Above all those are dismissive.
A feel of ethereal bliss,
Seductive, submissive and sensual
All in one in a cacophony,
Of ardent desire,
Plagued with fire.
Tempering with salutation
Of a prayer for dismal dainty eyes,
looking in hindsight,
For freedom far-sight.
Subsumed with eternal love,
Melting in the far horizon.

26. Fire Devil

A chrysanthemum so pure,

A cluster on the anvil.

Anvil of a show,

A flower show

Besieged with this "Fire Devil"

Causing a flutter.

A cluster of beauty and grace,

A fiery red,

Oh! What a watershed.

Alacrity to be subsumed in surrender

27. Bitter Sweet Bonsai

I am a prophecy of the past
To be stunted is my cast
To rise and affirm myself is the key
The colour's pink and lilac
Are, an incredible you…

28. Bottle Brush

Soft, serene and sensuous
A feast for the eyes
A delight for many
Surrendering to eternity
"Scarlet flower spikes"
A reverence to the sight
A tender touch
To hold and surrender
Come submit to eternal love.

29. A Horse Shoe

Oh! Horse Shoe

What a delight,

Come take me as an anchor

On your stride

You are the symbol of passive resilience.

A break in the stride

Like a symbol on strife

Oh! you are a delight

To a child's sight

A good luck charm

for the finders on tow,

Of a delight to sow

A seed for a sight

Paramount in hindsight

Come Dazzle and Dribble
with Children

30. Mesmerizing Mermaid

A folklore to tell,

Half woman half spell;

A thunder like a bolt

Bewitching, baffling

Oh! A call for love;

Setting Greece to the forefront

A splash in the sea

A Painters delight

A reader's paradise

Here is a femme fatale'

Venus is to the fore,

To herald an era of love,

While Amphitrite the goddess of the sea is here to stay.

At times they render boons

While at other times they leave us to fend for the storms

They are two coins of the same side.

31. A Sparkle

A thought

A provocation

Alas! An exploration.

A child at heart,

With a mind a head start.

Pure emerging as a prophesy of the past.

Waiting in the wings

A reality,

A recurrence waiting to decipher the reality,

Of a resurrection that is a restoration of serenity and simplicity that is sacrosanct

It is truly a sparkle in the eye

32. A Symphony of Love

She was beautiful in all guise'

With Caesar by her side;

Money was the name of the game.

This restored Caesar in Rome

In all richness that was like the Jewel in the crown;

Iconic Roman dictation

Oratory was at the back of his hand

Accolades came easy

He was the General who arose from the ashes

Striding on the high horse of fame and fortune

A born leader

Aligned with Queen of Egypt Cleopatra

On the penchant of love and lust

The assassination was a sad demise of a glorious era.

It was brutal Brutus who struck the final blow thus a friend who became a foe.

33. The Predicament of Whaling

Listen to the wail of the whale

Come let us sail away to capture the nuances of whaling

A harpoon shot like an arrow to start

A wail of the whale touching a chord in the heart;

The fin and the mink standing apart

Countries in the foray are Japan,

Norway and Iceland

Harpoon a high-powered rifle put to test

That does the trick

Oh! How? It takes a fall

The trauma needs to be capsized

Watch out for the ban on this game.

It is bounty brazen on the anvil of notoriety.

34. Playing Piano with Ivory

It is a game of chess

Check Mate

Check mate the use of Ivory on the bait

The queen foreplays in this enclave

She heralds the race against the pace

The piano in the orchestra comes to the fore

Demanding some sobriety in this show

Ivory! Ivory! Is the name of the game?

The symphony on the ride is put to shame

The piano key tops this race in frenzy

To put out s call on the ban

China and Hong-Kong

Is a prelude to this?

Stating loud and clear

The rise and fall to the prey of Ivory so dear

A prey to ornaments and medicines in a
mechanized way

Prevent poaching that is decay and debacle in all
that could be a miracle "Kimono" for Japan

A decorative glow

Rarer than money or gold

Etched in memory forlorn

It is head and tail two sides of the coin

The tusk is a high ride

Say No to Ivory.

Fact File

- Ban on Ivory trade came in 1989 under ICUN

- Attempt to stem killing

- Amendment of the Wildlife Protection Act Sale of domestic ivory banned on 23rd Nov 2022

- Ivory Act 2018 states that you cannot deal in items containing or made of elephant ivory

- Hong Kong largest market in the world

- China highest consumer of Ivory in the world for ornaments and medicine

- It used to be used as currency in olden times

- Used in Chess sets

- Karnataka highest quantity

- Thin veneer of piano key use to be made of ivory

- The differentiation is in the colour where ivory has a yellowish tint.

- The convention on international trade of endangered species (CITES) Bans Ivory Trade

- Today it is used for repair and refurbishment of the old keys.

35. Casper the Friendly Ghost

Pleasantness personified

Is the demeanor of the ghost?

Challenged by trio uncles

Came to the fore with animation in fore

Adventure through exploration

Mountain climbing, scuba diving and river rafting

A pursuit of knowledge

A home that is haunted

With fear as a personification

He set the pace in the race

Of friendship with mortals

He is chided on this path by a rooster a mole, a cat
and a mouse

Who take a mortified look?

Find friends among foes

Yes! He is none other than Fredie a fox cub who
turns into a ghost after life ends

His home is spooky

His name is Casper

He is the ruling rooster

An enigma of Boo! Boo!

Blowing the bugle coming to the fore with friends

A cartoon in all personification

Chugging like a comedian

Cartoon king on the zoom

Fact File

Look out for Casper's twin Jade who is his best friend

Legend has it that his mother drank a portion to have children Casper was born a ghost.

36. Black Black Bear

Black Black bear
What do you devour?
Huckleberries and blueberries
Don't feign a fright
As this is your new diet
Fruits and nuts
Seaweed a delicacy
A connoisseur's delight
The number on tentacle hooks
To their sensitive lips,
The moan and the groan
In subsuming the seeds
As a pulp
A gnawing hunger for food and fun
Heralding the age of seed dispersal
A pause to ponder
They have switched their dinner at the table.
A 'cherub' is born in full moon
Bringing joy surpassing noon
They fiery protect

Plunging in into an abyss
A cry in the forest for territory demarcated
A change from the Salmons delight
More berries please!

Fact File

- Encroachment on their territory

- Put your blinkers and spot the black bear

- Surmount the fear

- Climate change impacting their hibernation pattern

- Mamas Cherub" attempting to retaliate

- Shift to two-month hibernation due to melting of snowcapped mountains

37. Shooting Star

Oh! Look up into the sky
Do you see a fire?
Do you see friction?
In this journey forlorn
Where earth meets the sun
With the dust scattered around
A jubilation!
A Celebration above all
A good luck charm
Where east meets the west
Crying out for freedom
Waiting for Dawn
Waiting to surmount into the moonlit night
With a shooting star shining so bright
Like a catapult far from the heavens above
Watch out for this shooting star and make a wish.

38. A Teasing and Tantalizing Tulip

A cultivation, astride on the Turks

For some it was a pleasure while for some it was a mania

A besotted love,

Unconditional and

Devotional.

"Pink for happiness and confidence"

Purple striding on royalty

Yellow I hear you through loud cheers!

White a beckon for "Forgiveness"

May good fortune and fame be yours with the red one;

Yellow sunshine smile be yours in cheer!

Delightful dwellings all around

Are you a figment of my imagination or you route
the rooster in vein

May we fathom nature in all its bounty?

Come create the cacophony of colours for eternal love

Let us rejoice and resurrect the Tulip Mania of
the 17th century,

The Dutch "Golden age"

Fact File

It is also known as a speculative bulb in the Tulip Market

39. Pinocchio

Armed with a chiseled out of wood here in hindsight is Pinocchio the puppet by Geppetto.

The aspiration were worth welcoming…

Come see him as you watch the transformation of a young boy.

Liar put to test

A nose that grew leaps and bound as a deterrent for lying so the epic retold…

The roots were strong of the epic forlorn

Collodi describes him as a 'rascal'

An imp 'ragamuffin'

A thief in the making,

It is a call for alacrity to all this meandering

A playful puppet prone to lying

His journey was intriguing

Masquerading as a real boy

In the land of toys where sometimes he is a donkey
that could bray

At times joining in the antics of circus play

The woodpeckers are on the forefront

Nipping at his nose to bring some sobriety in this
creative exploration

Come take onus of responsibility

Fact file

- Pinocchio was a mascot at the first UEFA European Championship

40. A Plunge

One set to plunge

Two have a hunch

Three are a bunch

Four such a munch

Five on a tentacle flinch

Six penny for your thoughts

Seven dwarfs short and stout

Eight so much fun

Nine what a punch

Ten taking tepid tentative steps

41. Golliwog

Golliwog a designers delight;

A rag doll brought froth to life

Red rosy lips,

Black to the core

With frizzy hair in sight;

Golliwog black eyes,

Seductive by night,

In an array of stars shinning so bright;

A doll for many in might

A representative kinship by sight;

Looking for a friend amongst foe

A calling,

A custodian of human rights;

To disguise in all glamor

The white man to the shore;

Is it pure black or white?

Or a shade of grey in hindsight

The expanse like an arid desert

Is his calling a penchant?

Forbidden land "Ghoul" i.e. Ghost so to say

42. Day of the Dead Mexican Festival

Let us celebrate
The day of the dead;
We culminate,
We congregate,
Jubilation with
Fruit and flowers,
Resurrecting the dead.
Come etch every nuance
Without degrading the
Skull so fast
Go along with the rhythm
Adorning with affection
The colours so vast

Challenge the mood,
Melancholy and
Mastermind the past.

43. Flowers at a Fringe

A bird of paradise in a paradigm

A carnation in colours cajoling

Morning glory at mist

A pansy so pure

Tears for fears

A lily at leisure

A tuberose raising, hackles

Asters pink and purple in a cluster

A sunflower on the thrust of bloom at sunrise

Sweat pea a pod as a precursor to a thrust

Pansy in poise

Canary in a cast

Cycas revoluta is like a Craft

Flamingo on a fast

Fish tail propelling a fringe

A palm posing purity on a string

Orchids in an orchard

Christmas tree full in charisma

Red Rose in reign

Touch me not to stalk in surrender

With Jasmine in jive for a dive

Come Challenge the Debacles of the Mind

44. Monalisa a Stroke of a Brush

A genius so to decipher,

Leonardo de Vinci

An engineer,

An artist on the threshold of a smile

Cajoling Monalisa with a stalwarts delight

The enigmatic expression propelled with
monumental composition

Subtle yet becoming to the fore

Fondly known as Lisa

Highly esteemed and sought after

The incomparable Madonna

The smile a dilemma

The smile an effigy in other words the smile was a trick

A reflection of innocence

It was a reflection of renaissance embodiment of an ideal

Lurking in the wings is full of mystery and lure

Gautier compared Monalisa to a sphinx

A beauty, which smiles so mysteriously

The precarious shadow of a smile lurking in the background

'Subtle Smile'

45. Paul Cezanne

A French who chased a dream

A dream of being an artist,

Murals brought to the fore

Fathoming perfection through repetition was the name of the game;

He was gently prodded by Picasso and Matisse as "Father of us all"

Spring bringing flowers to the fore and

Summer masquerading in sunset.

Autumn full of zest

Winter bringing the chill oh! What, a thrill

Fondly known as "Ingres"

His style was romantic

Where he left a legacy both as a painter and as a portrait explorer.

He brought forth to his precursors of modern art to be etched in the works of Picasso and Matisse

His work got accolades

"Prix de Rome"

A challenge to his work style bizarre and archaic

"Raphaelesque" painting won acclaim,
a remembrance of Rapunzel let down your hair

Let perfection be lured through these turbulent test came stained windows, portrait of women in Turkish bath.

Nudity sinuous in all craft like a draft of fresh air

Turkish bath evocative

Through a harem in such a contrast

He was innovative trying to conquer his debacle of depression

He floated between the terms of "Madness"

Let us bring Van Gogh to the shore

Both sailing on a pristine show to the core

Van was a cut of the ear to drive away the demons from within while Cezanne was a loner putting himself to the test through destruction of his paintings.

Fact File:

- Like Van Gogh, his paintings were a reflection of his times through the eyes of Potato Eaters

- A man possessed with euphoria and despair

- There were bouts of crimson hues close his heart held feebly forming a link in the chain for creativity

- Look out for a basket of apples still life coming close to Potato eaters by Van Gogh

- Sight in motion by Cezanne

- Bathers Series

- Get knocked out by the pyramid of skulls

46. Reflections – William Wordsworth The Eternal Romantic

To a Butterfly

Fathoming courage from a chase and freedom to brush the dust off its wings

O Nightingale! Thou Surely Art

O Nightingale your song pierces through the stoic silence. You are indeed clinging on a grapevine for a plea so sure. Your voice is buried under the trees sheltered by the breeze. You cooed and cooed and on a after thought you wooed this time the penchant was for me.

At Furness Abbey

A strong clasp or clutch "to times prey" where ivy clings to sacred ruin to stall a "beautiful decay". Here is the stalking of the "Suns first smile" shines on a tall tower that is nothing but a debacle of debris.

I wondered lonely as a cloud:

I am a lonely cloud yearning to float around. I spot daffodils as golden as hay stack "dancing in the breeze". Look out for the twinkling of the star stretched away, dancing away the debacles in question in all elements that are here to stay. Hence for my heart is an echo comes forth to blend with the daffodils.

The Solitary Reaper:

In solitude she pleads for whispers in the dark
to be broken by a sickle as a shaft. She hears the
nightingale kneading a song of six pence. She lures
spring in chastity of a cuckoo bird breaking the
silence. Rise away the sorrow and pain. She blended
the sickle and it was a magical melody far so late'

My Heart Leaps:

A sight after a plight, to spot a rainbow in cue
after a strife

A benediction! A prayer and a restoration of a cycle
bound together in all piety.

To a Daisy:

A date with a daisy, to honor the poets, grave

A resurrection of hope,

To hold and to have!

An ache, to climb, the hills with assertion

To, sail on a stout ship.

The season made way for greens full of in all gaiety.

It was a delight; to the daisy flower in all sobrieties
he stole 'leisure hours'.

Ancient Wonders of the World – Come Preserve and Protect for Posterity

47. Great Wall of China

Come fathom the fort of china like phantom.
A protection against

Various, nomadic groups from the Eurasian Steppe

The wall is like a link chain built by Ming dynasty
and brought to the fore.

Simply put it is a "long wall"

Bringing fore defense to the core for emancipation
though a silk route.

Wall tower are like a stretch from Bohai Sea in the
east to the Gobi

dessert two thousand five hundred kilometers away
in the west.

48. Chichein Itza

Chichein Itza is a complex of mayan ruins on Mexico's Tucatan

Peninsula

A massive step pyramid known as Elcastillo or temple of

Kukulcan, dominates the ancient city.

Graphic stone carvings

Nightly sound and light shows illuminate the buildings

sophisticated geometry

It is reflective as a great civilization that it inhabited

It gets its name from cenote

It is an amalgamation of one huge pyramid cajoling smaller

pyramids within

Full of legend and lure to the fore

Legend has it that the serpent god Kukulkan descended on the

pyramid twice every year.

Also known as the temple of Kukulcan

El- Castillo

49. Petra – Jordan's Delight

Ancient Greece to the fore

Meaning a "rock"

It is an archeologist delight

Capital Of Nabataea Kingdom

Taking A Ride Via Narrow Canyon Called Al-Sid

A unique structure containing

'Tombs and Temples'

It is a might in sight

Pink stone to the throne

'Rose City"

A fortress in hindsight

Age notwithstanding the might

Stretched over 2150 years

A World Heritage to recon with

Carved from Cliffs

In Rome do as the Romans do

A jewel buried under sand as a temple

89

50. Machu Picchu

Old peak,

Old, mountain

Autodidactic

Stones cut to fit

Rays of the golden sun fall twice upon it

Also proclaimed as Temple of the Sun

Under the Inca dynasty

An archeologist delight

Brushed under the emblem so to say of the Heritage sight in 2020

51. Christ The Redeemer

A Statue depicting the Calm, courageous and
benevolent Christ in

Rio De Janero Brazil

Corcovado Mountain

Where beauty begets beauty a panoramic view

It was a miracle that the workers survived the height
on which the

statue was built

It commemorates Brazils independence from
Portugal

It was built in France by Paul Landovssk

It is a perfect pedestal peak

A threat as a debacle has been the striking of
lightning

A nine-year creative plunge of soap stone concrete

The mountain meets the mantle

Come view the miracle of man

It is Christo Redentor representing Latin America

Some call it a high-rise tribute to Catholicism

For others it is a salvo against secularism

A monument of science, art and religion.

52. Colossus of Rhodes

The remains lay on the ground for over eight
hundred years

Like a whip on a leash standing stoic

It is thought of as the sun god Helios

It is made of shaped bronze plates fastened to an
iron framework

A call for a hall of fame

A salutation

A benediction and a simple pledge for sustenance
of life

Time has stood still as Salvador Dali etched it on a
canvas frame

53. Taj Mahal in India

Forty thousand men oh! What a miracle

To a debacle

Fact File

- It is an epitome of love in resurrection of Anjumand Banu Begum fondly remembered as Mumtaz Mahal. A homage to the plight in fright for some.

- It is believed, that the hands, of the masons were amputated by Emperor Shah Jahan in an attempt to prevent another structure as the Taj Mahal to be re - created.

- A new york play by Rajiv Josephs "Guards at the Taj based on a myth"

Egypt to the Fore

54. The Great Pyramid of Giza

under the guise today

The largest Egyptian pyramid

It contains the tomb of Pharaoh Kufu

It is bound together with limestone and Granite

Oh! What a colossal sight.

Night comes to the shore in all elegance of
an anchor

An anchor on the boat

To travel through time and space

Resurrected as the Pharaoh's delight

On a conquest in hindsight

Of a seductive seclusion on this abode;

Two temples are temptations for the sight.

Calling for excursions by the night

One close, to the pyramid another by the Nile.

Tombs to the fore

A legend of "solar barges"

Where Sun God Ra used vessels in Egypt folk lure

55. A Legend of Tutankhamen's Curse

Time stood stoic in another era

Besieged by King Tut's curse

With death and destruction that came to the fore

For all who disturbed the Pharaoh in "eternal slumber"

The fore-runner was lord Carnarvon who succumbed to a bite by a mosquito

This was the entry point to the mummy's curse

To supplement this curse when lord Carnervon died "the lights in all Cairo went out" mysteriously.

The chase for beauty in bounty was eclectic in all grace and serenity.

It was a hall of fame.

A pharaoh put to rest in refinery exclaiming in wrath with the hope of avoiding dooms day

It was a resurrection from the past.

Age was no bar for the child Pharaoh who was discovered in the 'valley of kings'

In 1922

Nine was his chime in prime

Carter explored his tomb

Putting all to alacrity

A 'curse' a penchant of do or die.

Meandering of the treasure that was broken by high tides and hiccups

Was truly to restore the pharaohs might

Shielding him from the plight

Raiders were on the plunge.

But with foresight this monument was laid to test

To test by archeologist who ventured to understand the quest of mummification.

Come restore the myth of Tut's mummy

Take a detour to the grand Egyptian museum.

Gold embossed on wall

Gold on coffin;

Gold in a casket;

Sarcophagus of which the outer most was in red quartz (rock)

Fact File

- Stone coffin with sculpture

- Statues scintillating in the stark

- His mask in all sanctity of gold which heralded an era apart, for this boy king

- Who set the pace for an art

- King Tuts mother was queen Nefertiti and father Akhenaten

- A challenge for archeology would truly be a miracle to this debacle

- Nefertitis was a beckon for a bride on western civilization full of pride. The myth behind the tomb has yet to be resurrected.

57. The Sphinx of Giza

The sphinx was a symbol of protection of tombs and temples

Come explore.

Mythical creature

A face of a pharaoh Khafre

In all dignity the lion's body

In Giza Plateau on the banks of the river Nile

Red, blue and yellow a milieu of primary colours in a hue,

Red body,

Blue beard and

Yellow for headdress

Myth has it that the nose was chiseled to ward off evil.

One single limestone cut to perfection

It went chop! Chop! Chop!

Like the chisel of a sculpture in all dignity and sobriety

Legend has it that the Sun God protects its temple door.

Fact File

- Unlike the Greek, Sphinx is a woman the Egyptian is typically shown as a man.

- The Sphinx was created to guard the Pyramids and protect temples and tombs of Pharaohs

Conclusion – A Penchant for Peace

58. Five Elements of Nature to the Fore

'Pancha Mahaboot' in Sanskrit reflects "Five great
elements"

They are everywhere in the universe

Fire with might

Fire by delight

Sustenance in all propriety

Of knowledge and truth

Earth representing a stoic body and an eclectic soul
represented by the five senses

Come spot them

Day breaks with the shining aura of the sun

The aromatic tingle of senses with fragrance
of flowers

Eyes yearning for a vision of hope

Colours of a rainbow to the fore

Articulation an act of expression,

Taste the tingle of zest for a zing with lemonade

Ether is the fifth element

Aristotle noted it as a celestial sphere made of ether held the stars and planets.

Space a void to be filled with illusions

Artists design a holistic world through the elements of "line, shape, space, value, colour and texture

Water a salvation for self -clever as a fox through introspection.

A legend of Irma Lair – "control the fluidity of liquids.

Fact File

- There is an addition to the numbers of five elements with wood and Metal on an addition in this sacrosanct space.

- Wood in Chinese philosophy sometimes known as a tree is a life giver. It is a personification of warmth, generosity and cooperation

- Wood begets fire rub two pieces and ignite a spark

- Strong roots drawing energy from the soil

- Metal to question the purpose

59. Dawn of a New Day

She was a child;

She wore a smile

Mesmerizing her rise.

Her rise to an eloquent past;

Pride in her stride

To fight the strife;

Strife against Tyranny

Strife against drudgery and

Above all strife against inhumanity;

Strike terror against tyranny

Develop talent through rigorous training

In-cooperating generosity

Fathoming courage through engineering hope

Hence there is the dawn of a new day

Bright as a new day

A sunrise;

A dawn and

A dashing day that was an everlasting one…

Dedicated to Bharat Soka Gakkai – India

Bibliography

1. Singer Allan; illustrations, Pub: 1975 octopus books ltd 59 Grosvenor street London ISBN 07064049613 Printed in Hongkong

2. Wikipedia, Mermaid a symbol of love https://en.m.wikipedia.org

3. Chronicle of the queens of Egypt; Oct 2006; Cleopatra the last queen of Egypt

4. www.history.com

5. www.what life tours.com

6. Https:en.m.wikipedia.org.wikibritannicca

7. Truth about Whaling; Oct 22/2018

8. https://www.independent.co.uk-art

9. Isaacson Walter; The eyes and smile of Monalisa, pub: Oct. 19, 2017

10. Casper the friendly ghost; Wikipedia https://en.wikipedia.org

11. Fandom.com; Jade and Casper

12. Wordsworth. W; The eternal romantic; Random House Value Pub; 1996 ISBN - 0-51716109-5, Pub 1996, Brockhampton Press

13. http;//www.ramdomhouse.com

14. www.holland.com

15. www./mymodernmet.com

16. http/www.getty images.in

17. www.theguardian.com, june

18. http/the next crossing.com

19. http/www/Britannica.com

20. www.cancun-adventure.com

21. simple.n.wiki.org

22. Boorstein M; Colombia tribune.com

23. Murphy Johanna, wwf, 29/12/10

24. The story of Shah Jahan; urban myth/folk lore

25. UNESCO Heritage 7/7/2020

26. https/en.m.wikipedia.org; A puppeteers delight

27. www.bloomandwild.com

28. https/wwwsaraheaven.com.articles

29. history of tulip flower 14 dec.2020

30. https/symbolstage.com-symbolisation

31. https/bear.or-berries.acritical

32. https/www.bearsmart.com-food

33. J.K. Policy institute commentaries 28 Aug 2020

34. Hameed Adeela; survival of Himalayan Black Bear, hinges on human life

35. National Geographical Society History of Ivory Trade

36. Https/www.national Geo-org; 27th Sept 2022

37. https/www.poaching facts.com

38. https/www.gov.uk.guidance

39. Everettpianoservices.com

40. Tyldesley Joyce; Tutankhamers Curse; - Britannica

41. www.britanicca

42. www.history for kids.net